3302378491

Peter

..ocks, Women's Hostel
buildings.

nd first fatalities

eing on 1 April 1918 and No. 28
n (TDS) was formed at Weston
of 21st Wing on 27 July as a
aining unit, and it is assumed
ning date for the airfield. TDSs
lly 1917, usually by the merger
drons (TS) on the same station
·y were No. 61 TS at South
and No. 70 TS at Beaulieu,
quipment were two seat Avro
le seat Sopwith Camel fighters
later replaced with the new
h Salamanders which were just
luction line. At its peak the
e 36 Salamanders and 36 Avro
before Weston claimed its first
1 17 August Camel C1660 spun
itt when he was practicing rolls
l on 26 September, Canadian,
t suffered the same fate when
) ft (1524 m) in Camel C1612
vertical turns, crashing near
on.

s the fate of 2nd Lt E S Scott
from his aircraft, possibly a 504,
n the 13th A/Sgt S Bolton lost
ed during an inverted flat spin
One Camel, F1400, had
a France having claimed two
h the 148th US Aero Sqn. but
graph wires and spun in on 24
injuring Capt DTM Kenmard.
d and force landed from 20 ft

included 5 double General Service Flight Sheds, an
Aeroplane Repair Section Shed, a Plane Stores, a
Salvage Shed, Technical Stores, Power House,
Vehicle Sheds, Workshops, Offices, Regimental
Institute and Stores, Officers' Mess, N.C.O.s' Mess,

(0.1 m) on 9 December after engine failure injuring
its pilot 2nd Lt. CF Purdy. Sadly, fatal accidents were
not uncommon at training establishments, and
continuing into 1919 on 16 January 2nd Lt J A
Humphrey with pupil, Flt Cadet H Begg, spun in

Above: 2 Sqn moved in from Bicester with FK.8s in September 1919
(Author's collection)

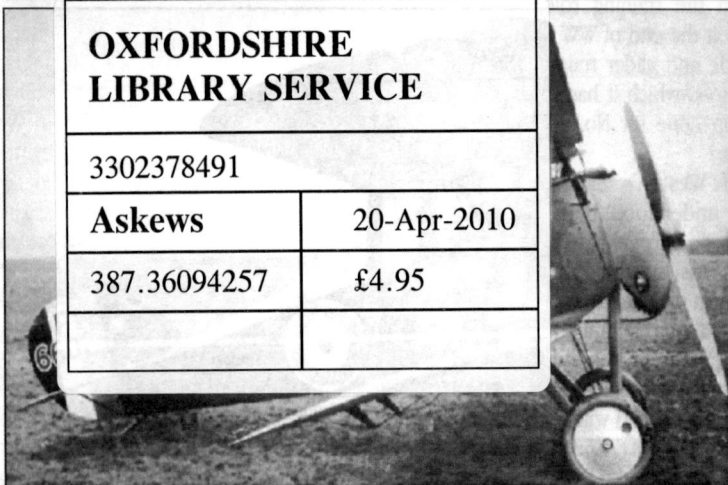

Left: The Sopwith Salamander replaced the Camels with 28 TDS
(Author's collection)

after take off in an Avro 504, 25 year old Humphrey being the only fatality. Only six days later his namesake, 2nd Lt AG Humphrey, lost his life when he stalled in after an engine failure during a spin in Camel F9608 and on the 30th,19 year old Flt Cadet M J Hefferman died when his Camel F9617 came out of a half-roll too low and flew into the ground. Humphrey and an E S Scott are buried in St. Mary's Churchyard at Weston-on-the-Green and G B Scott and Willscroft are buried at Botley Cemetery near Oxford.

In service a few Camels were modified locally as duel control trainers and one such, C68, was at Weston by December 1918. Other identified Camels were B7337, C69, C8301, E1530, F6375, F6383 and F6387. The foregoing details have been gleaned from Air-Britain's The Camel File, the 504s

and Salamanders not having such detailed histories to refer to. 28 TDS survived until March 1919 when, like many similar establishments, it was disbanded and it was not until September that aircraft were again seen in the skies around Weston when two front line squadrons became based. 2 Sqn. had travelled the short distance from Bicester, equipped with two seat Armstrong Whitworth F.K. 8 reconnaissance biplanes and remained until disbanding on 20 January 1920 and 18 Sqn. moved in from Merheim, Germany in name only, only to disband on 31 December, later reforming at nearby Upper Heyford in October 1931 with Hawker Harts.

Any aircraft which remained on the airfield after its closure were stripped of any useful components and the airframes sold as scrap. In 1919 the village

Two views of the Avro 504, which was the basic trainer when 28 TDS formed at Weston in July 1918. *(Authors collection)*

speculate that this could be the connection. These fuselages remained in place until the sixties when we will take up their story again.

Closure and advertised for disposal

During 1919 the Surplus Government Property Disposal Board advertised that Surplus Plant, Building Material and two locomotives at Weston-on-the-Green and Bicester would be put up for auction by Messrs Buckell & Ballard, an auction to take place at Weston on 30 September and at Bicester on the following three days. An advert in the *Oxford Chronicle* for 27 August 1920, stated that the Board was considering disposing of the airfield as a whole, *"or of the buildings and the land on which they stand without the landing ground"* but the buildings were not for sale for removal from the site. It was suggested that the buildings might be suitable for conversion into a hospital, convalescent home, sanatorium, training institution or for housing. It

wheelwright Mr H Boddington purchased some Bristol F.2B Fighter fuselages and wings for a few shillings for re-roofing his workshop and making fences. The origins of these aircraft remains a mystery as the type was not used at Weston but after disbanding 2 Sqn reformed at Oranmore, Ireland on 1 February equipped with the type and one can

Above: Two pilots in an ground vehicle with 'SEA 28 TDS Weston 6T' RAF identity on left door. *(Authors collection)*

Right:Chequered Camel C1660 was the aircraft in which 2nd Lt Bertram Scott died when he spun in on 17 August 1918. *(via Mike Gibson)*

Right: 2nd Lts E S Scott and J A Humphrey lie at rest in St Mary's churchyard in Weston-on-the-Green and the wreath against Scott's headstone in November 2006 is evidence that they are not forgotten *(Author's collection)*

Below: World War One buildings - thought to have originally been warehouses - opposite main gate in 2007 *(Author)*

Below: Another World War One building - possibly a Mess - opposite airfield in 2007 *(Author)*

Left: A posed Weston shot, possibly late '20s, with a hangar wall in the background. *(via Mike Gibson)*

also noted that there were permanent macadam roads, a water-borne drainage system, a water supply and that electricity was generated on site. At around the same time similar ads appeared in the local press for Upper Heyford and Witney. Although some buildings had been dismantled, during the twenties and thirties some families took up residence on the domestic site. With the disbandment of 2 Sqn, all flying activities on the airfield of any

Superb vertical taken from the west on 17 March 1930 illustrating the remnants from the first war. The base of the double GS shed can be seen on the left and the walls of the ARS and the other two double GS sheds remain standing *(via John Norris)*

significance seems to have ceased, or not yet come to light, for almost twenty years. It had returned to agriculture by 1922, being used for grazing, and there was a quarry at the north-west corner of the field.

Oxford Gliding Club beginnings

It is not known when The Oxford Gliding Club (OGC) started operating from the airfield but it is on record that in 1930 they became the first club the country to try out the towing of gliders behind vehicles after seeing an article on this method of launching being carried out in America. A Zogling glider was used with about 450 ft (137.2 m) of rope which gave launches to around 250 ft (76.2 m). The Oxford Times for 7 November 1930 recorded *"At Weston-on-the-Green on Sunday, crowds gathered on the aerodrome site to watch the Oxford Gliding Club practice. A car chassis was used for towing the glider across the course and it gave excellent "take-offs".* It also recorded that *"on many of the flights the length of the aerodrome was covered before landing and that a succession of flights was*

In the left background of this 1930 photo of an anonymous group of horsemen on the airfield is the remains of a brick buttress from one of the dismantled General Service Sheds *(via John Norris)*

Yes, we know it's not a good picture, but this was taken from a microfilm recording the *Oxford Mail* for 3 November 1930 of the Oxford Gliding Club Zogling glider which was launched behind a car. *(Author's collection)*

made also on Saturday afternoon." This is the earliest recorded mention of the OGC that the author has come across but the club went on to operate from Cumnor Meadow and Aston Rowant pre-war and Kidlington post-war prior to the move to Weston in 1956, where they still reside.

By the mid-thirties all that was left of the hangars were the brick pillars which had supported the roofs and these were put to good use as a backdrop in 1936 when Alexander Korda shot some sequences for his futuristic film *"Things to Come"* which was being filmed at Denham Studios, some villagers taking part as extras, being paid 5s for a day on the set. On 17 December 1937 a 90 Sqn. Blenheim K7052 from Bicester crashed just north of the airfield while on fuel consumption trials.

With the onset of war extra land was taken over for extending the airfield and until accommodation was built near the airfield some air and ground crew were accommodated in the village, those more fortunate in The Ben Johnson Inn and others had to travel the 6 miles (9.65 km) to RAF Bicester.

Powered flying returns after a break of almost twenty years

It was not until the threat of war was looming in Europe that the airfield again saw any serious aircraft movements when possibly the first powered aircraft to operate out of Weston since the early twenties were Fairey Battles when 142 Sqn. from neighbouring Bicester moved in for a week from 6 to 12 August 1939 for Air Defence Exercises. War was declared on 3 September and the next to visit

were Bristol Blenheims of 90 and 101 Sqns. from RAF West Raynham, Norfolk on the 7th having received orders to 'scatter' from their home base to avoid being caught on the ground by surprise enemy attack from the air. 101 moved on to Brize Norton on the 14th and 90 to Upwood on the 19th. To relieve active squadrons of their training tasks, in 1939 it was decided to set up a number of Group Pools, withdrawing some squadrons from their operational roles and designating them as training units. 104 and 108 Sqns. took up residence at Bicester in mid-September, both equipped with Blenheim Is, IVs and Ansons. Both were Group Training Squadrons tasked with training crews for operational squadrons, Bicester becoming No. 2 Group Pool, under the control of 6 Group, to supply light day bomber crews for its Norfolk based front line Blenheim squadrons. Weston became Bicester's Relief Landing Ground (RLG) and both the Ansons and Blenheims trained from here and sadly 108 Sqn. lost Ansons N5158 and N5177 when they were involved in a mid-air collision close to the airfield on 31 October.

Terrible weather conditions prevailed through the winter months but by December Weston was also used for bombing practice and during the month, due to flooding at Bicester, all flying was transferred to Kidlington. Flying was again curtailed for long periods due to flooding or heavy snow falls for the first three months of 1940. In April, Group Training Pools were converted to Operational Training Units (OTUs), the squadrons being reformed as operational units elsewhere, 104 and

Blenheim 1 of 90 Sqn., Bicester came to grief north of the airfield on 17 December 1937. (D.S.W. Blee collection)

108 Sqns. merging to become 13 OTU in 6 (Training) Group on the 8th, with an establishment of 36 Blenheims and 12 Ansons, Weston remaining as the unit's RLG, used mainly for night flying. May and June were blessed with very good weather, 3700 hours being flown during June alone, by which time an additional twelve Blenheims and four Ansons had joined the unit.

In July Upper Heyford based 16 OTU was making use of the airfield as on the 5th Handley Page Hampden L4142 ended up in a ditch after landing and on the 19th a Napier Dagger engined variant of the Hampden, Hereford L6026 suffered a starboard engine fire after take-off from its base due to the failure of a big-end bearing and force landed at Weston where the fire was extinguished thanks to the prompt action by the fire crew which was on detachment from Bicester. The following day a 16 OTU aircraft was again in trouble when Hampden P4296 ran into soft ground on landing and the undercarriage collapsed.

Weston becomes Oxfordshire's first casualty of the Luftwaffe

Evident of the intense training activities in the local area and vulnerability of trainee crews often flying age weary aircraft, just after midnight on the night of 8-9 August 13 OTU Blenheim 1 L1191 lost control on approach, dived into the ground and burnt killing the three Sgt crew members, Nelson, Sanderson and Smith. Also on that day Weston received unwelcome notoriety when it became the first airfield in Oxfordshire to receive attention from the enemy when late that night a stick of 16 High Explosive (HE) bombs were dropped over a two mile line from Chesterton to the landing ground, five of the bombs exploding on the airfield but caused little damage.

With the Battle of Britain at its height, on the night of 25/26 August, the Luftwaffe again visited, this time dropping 16 HE bombs and around 140 incendiaries, again without any serious damage.

Upper Heyford 16 OTU Hampdens were using the airfield by the summer of 1940. *(Author's collection)*

Weston was Bicester's RLG for 13 OTU Blenheims on its formation in April 1940. *(Author's collection)*

Quite what the Luftwaffe thought was going on at Weston is not clear but more bombs were dropped on the field the following night leaving the lads another seven holes to fill in. On 1 September three bombs made direct hits on Bicester's dummy airfield at Grendon Underwood and on the night of 2/3 September five HEs were dropped near the airfield and more on the nearby Otmoor bombing range. This action continued on the 4th when three delayed action bombs were dropped on the airfield, followed by three more on the 6th when the airfield was declared unserviceable, remaining out of action for four days. Bombs continued to be dropped in the neighbourhood of Bicester on several occasions throughout September and October, some just to the north of Weston on the night of 3/4 October and to the south-east on 24 October.

13 OTU was having a bad spell of accidents at Weston as on 28 September F/O Sharp took-off at 2150 in Blenheim L6781 on his first night solo on the type, climbed too steeply, stalled and crashed into some trees. The aircraft caught fire on impact but Sharp escaped without serious injury. On 21 October after take-off at 1420 Blenheim L8871 suffered an engine cut causing it to swing out of control and crash, killing Sgts Hillelson and Kerr on impact, Sgt Dismore dying of his injuries two days later. On the 25th another of the type, Z5804, undershot on a night approach, hit trees and crashed, the pilot escaping without injury.

Blenheims and Ansons move out – Harvards and later Oxfords move in

13 OTU Ansons and Blenheims continued to use Weston as an RLG until 1 November 1940 when the newly completed and more suitable RAF Hinton-in-the-Hedges took over the role. On that day Weston changed its allegiance and continued in the same role with 15 Service Flying Training School (SFTS) at nearby Kidlington, which was equipped with Harvards, primarily for night flying, and by the middle of the month 'J' and 'K' Flights of 'B' Sqn. had moved in. It was not long before this unit suffered its first casualty at Weston as on the 14th Harvard 1 N7089 undershot and hit a tree on a night approach and crashed. Only nine days later Harvard P5828 flew into the ground 1.5 miles (2.4 km) south of the airfield when on a night approach and on the 25th another of the type, P5888, hit a hedge on approach to land. A tragic accident took place at 18.35 on 7 December when 16 OTU Hampden P4292 attempted a forced landing after an engine failure when night flying but rolled and dived into the ground at nearby Chesterton with the loss of five crew.

15 SFTS initially trained Group I (single engine) pilots but its role changed to training Group II (twin engine) pilots in January 1941 and it re-equipped with Airspeed Oxfords. Recently delivered Oxford L9696 flew into the ground during a night landing in fog on 11 February 1941 and another, R6158, failed to climb after a night take-off with the wrong fuel

mixture setting and hit a pole on 21 March. Sadly, accidents were the only happenings of note; and on 16 April Oxford V3645 crashed after stalling on take off; P9043 flew into the ground during a night take-off on the 21st and R6154 and R6378 collided over the airfield on 27 May. Visiting 16 OTU Anson N9578 hit a bus with a wingtip on 2 July and Oxford V3956 had an engine cut on take-off, hit a hedge and dived into the ground on 30 August. Allister Fraser recalled that initially ground crew would travel from Kidlington to Weston to carry out maintenance on the Oxfords, which would fly there each afternoon, carry out night flying, and return about 10 a.m. the following morning when they would get breakfast in

a cafe opposite the main gate. At first Allister was lucky enough to be put up at the Ben Johnson pub while others were put up in local houses. When they arrived were no facilities but soon after contractors started erecting a blister hangar, tents were put up as the technical offices and the troops assisted in erecting a Nissan hut for a billet which they moved into a couple of weeks later. Another task was to guard the recognition beacon situated in a field a few miles away.

Losses to enemy action

The Luftwaffe scored against soft targets on the night of 12 August when the pilot (believed to have

This 7 July 1941 shot from a 15 FTS Oxford shows the original main gate and black bitumen painted camouflage hedge lines across the landing ground, which strangely do not follow the pattern of hedge lines in surrounding fields. (*via John Norris*)

From another 7 July shot, two Oxfords can be seen as well as crop-marked World War One features and the well established 1918 domestic site west of the Oxford to Brackly road. *(Via John Norris)*

been Ofw. Rolf Bussmann) of a Ju 88 joined the night flying Oxfords, shooting down R6156, which crashed near Sturdy's Castle, a public house on the Banbury road north of Kidlington, killing its Norwegian pilot Flt. Sgt. Julin-Olsen, and within minutes, W6629, which crashed near Weston-on-the-Green village with the loss of student pilot LAC C P Blair. The Ju 88 then strafed the airfield damaging seven Oxfords before returning to its Gilze Rijen, Holland base. 13 OTU Blenheim Z5804 undershot on a night landing, hit a tree and crashed on 25 October and a 15 SFTS Oxford N6433 crashed after overshooting on15 November, killing the pilot.

Glider training takes over

Towards the end of 1941 Dominions trained aircrews had started arriving in Britain and it was decided that all basic flying training would take place overseas within the Empire Air Training Scheme. During the summer space had become at a premium at Ringway (now Manchester Airport), home of the Glider Training Squadron which had formed the previous September and in August, when glider training became a necessity for the airborne forces, accommodation for new training units had to be found and the Squadron transferred to Thame, Bucks in December. This unit survived for a year and on 1 December 1941 disbanded to form Nos. 1 and 2 Glider Training Schools (GTS) which were established with General Aircraft Hotspur training gliders and Hawker Hector biplane glider tugs coming under No. 70 Group Army Co-operation Command. Three days later AOC in C Flying Training Command and AOC 23 Group visited both Kidlington and Weston to discuss the immediate formation of a GTS at Weston and it was decided to transfer the newly formed 2 GTS to the airfield without delay. The opening-up party arrived from Thame on 8 December and to get the School under way, ten Hectors, eleven Hotspurs, 58 parachutes and 30 tow ropes were requested on the 10th December and the unit was in place by the 12th. During 1942 three further training schools were formed; No. 3 at Stoke Orchard, Glos and Nos. 4 and 5 at nearby Kidlington.

On the 13th a Fairey Battle from RAF Netheravon was trialled as a tug but was rejected as being unsuitable and on the 17th duel control Hind, K5450, was taken on charge. On arrival, 2 GTS had an establishment of 30 Hotspurs (A and B Flights), one Hawker Hind trainer, 16 Hector tug aircraft and two De Havilland Tiger Moths and additional covered accommodation was provided by the erection of several canvas Bessoneau hangars. The Hotspur had been designed as an assault glider able to carry a pilot and seven troops but did not meet operational requirements and was relegated to training duties. The layout for the new hangars was decided by Army Co-operation Command but 15 SFTS objected as the siting would seriously interfere with the approach to the flare path in a prevailing wind and after consultation they were relocated and erected between the 9th and 16th December.

On 22 December, 2 GTS was transferred to 23 Group, Flying Training Command and the first three Hectors arrived, being joined by another five by the end of the month. There were to be 12 glider instructors and nine tug pilots to train pupils on the Hotspur gliders during six week courses, commencing at three week intervals. During the first full month of training 16 pupils were being trained as tug pilots and another 16 as glider pilots, eight pupils having completed their gliding course with 1 GTS being posted in for tugging instruction. With 2 GTS already functioning, on 23 December 'J' and 'K' Flights of 15 SFTS returned to Kidlington and Weston ceased to be its RLG, although the airfield was still used for night flying as on 11 January 1942 Oxford R6179 collided with parked Hector K9785, ending its career and on 10 February, Oxford P1092 swung during an attempted night overshoot, hit a hangar and crashed. 101 (Glider) OTU formed at Kidlington in January and 15 SFTS, which was now the only such unit providing pilots for night fighter OTUs made the move north to Leconfield, Yorkshire in February.

Four Hotspurs arrived by road from No. 15 Maintenance Unit, Wroughton, Wilts on the 26th December, a Tiger Moth from Haddenham on the 29th and eight Hector tugs had arrived by the 31st, of which four were loaned to 1 GTS, Thame in exchange for two dual Hectors and two solo Hectors without towing hooks for use on the conversion course for new tug pilots. By 1 January 1942 2 GTS had the following aircraft:

Hector Tugs	K8140, K8161, K8166, K9718 (loaned to 1 GTS) K8111, K8143 (damaged at Thame), K9706, K9785
Hector Duel Tug	K8126, K9734 (on loan from 1 GTS)
Hector Solo	K8162, K9744 (loaned from 1

Groundcrew preparing tow cable as Hotspur BT600/I waits to launch *(via John Norris)*

A trio of Hotspurs including /I and /O approach to land. (via John Norris)

	GTS)
Hind (duel)	K5450
Tiger Moth	N9197, T5628
Hotspurs	BT602, BT603, BT604, BT605
	(not yet assembled)
	BT542, BT543 (loaned from 1
	GTS)

A Hawker Audax, two-seat Army Co-operation biplane was trialled as a glider tug and was found more suitable than the Hector and the establishment was amended to 16 of the type.

1942 got off to a bad start when 2 GTS Tiger Moth T5628 stalled in haze and side slipped into the ground near Kirtlington on 8 January, the pilot escaping unhurt, and three days later Oxford R6179 ran into Hector tug K9785 on the ground. On the 15th a PR Spitfire landed in bad weather, damaging the undercarriage. In early February the runways were widened to 75 ft (22.8 m) and some walls were dismantled. It was found that with favourable weather conditions 70 to 80 tows per day were within the units' capability and the 2nd course commenced on 11 February and the first was completed on the 17th. On the 16th Hampden P1177 of 16 OTU mistook Weston for Upper Heyford during a night cross country and force landed at 2030, luckily without harm to the crew.

The first glider incident occurred on the 23rd February when Hotspur BT718 lost its canopy and subsequently lost control and crashed near the airfield, the pilot escaping with bruises.

During March Audax began to be replace the Hectors, five arriving on the 7th, although a few were retained for full-load towing duties. There was a Royal visit on 3 March when the Duke of Kent was a guest of the unit. Hector tugs were still coming on charge as K8126 was received on 8 March and on 11 April it descended through low cloud and flew into the ground 0.5 mile (0.8 km) SW of the airfield, killing the pilot. On 6 May Hotspur BT561 stalled on the tow and flew into the ground and on the 18th BT674 hit the ground when turning in to land and overturned. The unit Senior Engineering Officer visited the Miles factory at Woodley on 4 April, to discuss release of Master two-seat advanced trainers for use as tugs. During the month the airfield was camouflaged and two new blister hangars completed and by the middle of the year a peritrack had been laid and a watch office and new hangars erected. Another accident occurred on 6 May when Hotspur BT561 climbed too steeply on tow-off and crashed killing the pilot and on the 17th the duel Hind K5450 burst a tyre on landing, swung and tipped on its nose.

Kidlington based 102 (Glider) OTU made use of

Left: An Army Corporal deplanes from a Hotspur while an RAF pilot and Army Sergeant look on.

Below: Pleasing photo of Hotspur approaching to land *(both via John Norris)*

the airfield for night flying during May, one of their Hectors, K8151, bouncing on landing and its undercarriage collapsing on 20th. New workhorses were the order of the day for 2 GTS when the first three Master II tugs arrived from the Woodley factory on the 28th. By the end of June another three had arrived and all tug pilots had been converted to the type and in July another 50 tug pilots were posted in for conversion to the Master II. Also during June 296 Sqn. visited from Netheravon with Hectors towing troop laden Hotspurs for tactical exercises.

No. 10 Elementary Flying Training School at Weston-Super-Mare disbanded on 21 July and its personnel were transferred to 2 GTS for glider experience prior to becoming the nucleus of No 3 GTS which formed at Stoke Orchard, Gloucestershire on the same date. On the 26th Hotspur BT685 lost its tailplane due to structural failure in flight and crashed _ mile (0.84 km) SW of the airfield with the loss of the two occupants, on the 31st Hector K8142 swung on landing and tipped up and on 10 August a Master on take-off collided with a Hotspur being towed by a tractor and one

Hotspurs BT551/L and /N on approach.

Below: Hotspur /J about to touch down (both via John Norris)

man was killed. Another, DL305 was written off on the 25th when it was hit by DL369 which was taking off and four days later Hotspur BT594 lost its tow on take off and crashed on the airfield. A new establishment was for 40 Masters and 60 Hotspurs but by the end of August only 22 Masters were on strength, During the summer training was taking place at No. 1 Satellite Landing Ground at Slade Farm, which was about 3 miles (4.8 km) NW of the airfield, Master DL307 coming to grief there on 1 July and on 20 August at the same location Hotspur BT551 was written off after being towed-off without a pilot! During the year a two storey watch office of temporary construction was erected but any further details have not been found.

On 2 September Master tug DL425 towing Hotspur HH518 crashed into the spire of St. Mary's church in Witney, Sgt Couch and LAC Rodger both suffered fatal injuries; an MO and ambulance from RAF Brize Norton attended. A ground accident on the 18th proved fatal for an AC2 when he was struck buy a landing glider and died shortly afterwards. A record number of 1012 tows were recorded for week ending 24 September and on that day Master DL516 stalled when towing Hotspur BT624, both aircraft crashing at Chesterton with the loss of two lives and Master DL432 undershot during a night landing and overturned on 7 October. By April, Upper Heyford's 16 OTU had exchanged its tired Hampdens and Herefords for Wellingtons and these also became occasional visitors to Weston, BK214 overshooting on landing on 6 December causing some minor damage. In December 2 GTS took over the running of RAF Thame which was still home to the Glider Instructors School but this task was short lived as the unit disbanded on 31 January 1943 and

Above: A loose formation of Hotspurs with Audax tugs NW of the airfield.

Right: 2 GTS No 3 (Army) Refresher Course group photo with Major Roe, fourth from left on front row.
(both via John Norris)

2 GTS 30th March 1942 group with General 'Boy' Browning centre posed in front of Hawker Hector tug (via John Norris)

Above: Eleven Hotspurs, four Audax and an Anson are seen in this shot, possibly the visit of HRH The Duke of Kent on 3 March 1942. *(via John Norris)*

In late May 1942 2 GTS received its first Miles Master II tugs which eventually replaced the Hector and Audax biplanes *(via W J Bushell)*

A course passing-out parade with Army officer awarding wings as an RAF officer watches on. *(via John Norris)*

the airfield was put to other uses. Another cold and wet winter had left Weston's surface unfit and on 1 February a detachment transferred to Cheddington where it remained until 20 March and during the month some flying was again carried out at Slade Farm and Weston flying field was harrowed.

Oxfords return

Its task completed, 2 GTS was disbanded on 10 March 1943, followed by Nos 1 GTS at Croughton and 4 GTS at Kidlington on the 23rd, to provide personnel for No. 20 (Pilots) Advanced Flying Unit (PAFU) which formed at Kidlington on the same day with an establishment of 37 Oxfords. Former 2 GTS Master DL472 spun in on the airfield on 26 March and by then may have been on the strength of 20 PAFU which also had a mixed bag of support aircraft and those that may have visited Weston were Anson,

Gull Six, Hind, Proctor and Tiger Moth after Weston became its RLG on 6 April and remained so until it disbanded 22 months later. The Oxfords mainly operated from Weston but until the end of July day and night flying was also carried out at the units Kingston Bagpuize, Berkshire RLG and during this period Oxfords, Hotspurs and Master tugs were operated. On 11 May Oxford N4599 stalled on approach and crashed and six days later, another of the type, T1100, stalled on landing, bounced and tore its undercarriage off. Summerfield Track, which was a temporary surface comprising a woven wire chain-link mesh, with metal rods threaded transversely, was laid in September and no doubt the waterlogged state of the airfield the previous winter was the reason for this.

In 1943 it was noted that there were four Bessonneau hangars of canvas and wood construction and eight Blisters of various types which were small arched metal covered buildings. There were windsocks at the NE and W boundaries and a landing T was positioned outside the watch office and flying control was undertaken by the duty pilot and met facilities were provided by RAF Kidlington. 2,400 gals (10910 l) of aviation fuel were available, refuelling was by bowser and the MT section held 1,000 galls (4546 l) for its vehicles. There were seven tractors for aircraft movements and recovery of gliders and two Johnson tractors for use as snow ploughs or rolling the airfield and for aircraft recovery or engine changes there was a pair of shear legs and jibs on tractors. As it was a grass field there was no permanent lighting and for night flying a flare path was used. In reserve for emergency use were 24 tons (24.38 t) of bombs and 390,000 rounds for anti-aircraft use. Additional land had been added during the war as the airfield dimensions were now N – S 1100 yds (1005.8 m), NE – SW 1330 yds (1216 m), E – W 1,600 yds (1463 m) and SE – NW 1,200 yds (1097 m). A noted landmark by day was the Oxford to Bicester railway line 1.5 miles (2.4 km) SE and by night a lake 1 mile (1.6 km) WSW. The RAF manning establishment on 1 December 1944 was 47 officers, 216 SNCOs and 434 other ranks, plus 8 WRAF officers and 126 other ranks.

After an accident free period the rescue crews were again called into action on 6 March 1945 when 20 PAFU Oxford P1926 lost an engine during an overshoot and crashed 1 mile (1.6 km) north of the

An anonymous group of 20 (P)AFU ground crew pose in front of Oxford 'FF' with canvas Bessoneau hangar in background
(via John Norris)

airfield, the run of luck now broken, on 1 April Oxford, BG574, stalled on take-off and crashed. On 21 June the PAFU was disbanded and flying ceased at Weston and the airfield was officially closed down on 21 June when the instructional aircrew were posted to Kidlington. With the RAF now having a glut of aircrew, holding centres were formed around the country where they would await their disposal, No. 1 Air Crew Holding Unit being formed in 23 Group at Kidlington on 14 June with a detachment at Weston until it disbanded on 1 October. Less Jubbs, an Australian, was one of the many recently graduated commonwealth pilots that arrived in the UK during 1944 only to find that they were surplus to the needs of the RAF. He then had to wait a year before being posted to Weston for his advanced flying course and the war came to an end in Europe while he was there. All RAF pilots left the course but the Australians remained as the Pacific war was still not won.

With reference to the 1945 site plan a T2 hangar had been erected on the airfield side of the technical site, which remains in use today, and there were two nine bay Bessonneaus and four over, two extra over and five extra over double Blister hangars. There were four dispersed sites and the communal site with the messes with their own sewage works alongside the A4095 road NW of the airfield, west of the Oxford to Brackley road. The Main Gate to the airfield was located further north along the road from the one currently in use and this may have changed in the late forties. The entrance is still there, but closed off by a metal gate and the guardroom and nearby buildings have long since been demolished.

An interesting aside concerning the airfield is mentioned by David Smith in his *Britains Military Airfields 1939 – 1945*. As war was drawing to a close consideration was given to building a national aeronautical research establishment, similar to that at Muroc in California that would involve a huge tract of the English countryside being taken over. Eight existing airfields that could be extended to take an 8000 yd (7315 m) runway were considered and Weston was one of these but needless to say the idea was dropped.

Above: Taken on the day war ended, Aussie Flt. Sgts. Back row Snowy Eldridge, Eddie Stanbury, Les Jubbs; front row Peter Cooney, Roy Mulligan, Redge Smith and Al Baker *(Les Jubbs)*

Left: A group of 20(P)AFU Aussies at Weston in 1945 *(Les Jubbs)*

A "clueless formation" of 20(P)AFU Oxfords in 1945 *(Les Jubbs)*

Parachutists take over

On 1 October 1945 the Station was transferred to Maintenance Command and it became a sub-site of No. 3 Maintenance Unit at Milton near Didcot, Berkshire which dealt with ground equipment until it disbanded on 31 December 1947. 16 OTU remained at Upper Heyford until March 1946 when it moved to Cottesmore, Rutland making way for the Station to have a complete change in role,

transferring to 38 Group, Transport Command on the 15th. The Parachute Training School (PTS), which had formed at Ringway, Cheshire in February 1942 and was redesignated as No 1 PTS in July 1944 made the move south and took up residence at Upper Heyford on 28 March, taking control of Weston as its Dropping Zone (DZ). It came with its own Dakota, Halifax, Wellington and Oxford transport aircraft, a 70 ft (21.3 m) training tower and

With Dakotas the Halifax made the first para drops at Weston on 15 May 1946 (1 PTS)

A 1 PTS Halifax drops another course of pupils over Weston in 1946 (1 PTS)

kite balloons. The first parachute descents were made at Weston on 15 May when there were ten from a Halifax and 11 from a Dakota. In the meantime tethered Kite balloons had arrived at Weston and were put to use two days later. Amazingly, 6 decades on the station is still under the control of 1 PTS and remains as its DZ.

Trainees made their initial jumps from the tower at Upper Heyford and then from one of two kite balloons moored at Weston and when proficient they went on to jump from a Halifax Mk.VIII or a Dakota onto the Weston DZ. At this time 1 PTS was responsible for training replacements for the Parachute Regiment and the first Territorial Army recruits which were just coming onto the scene. On 3 December 1947 1 PTS took over the task of glider

Taken on 16 April 1947, this interesting shot shows the still intact four dispersed sites, the communal and sewage sites 1.5 miles (2.4 k) NW of the airfield. *(Author's collection)*

training and was redesignated as No. 1 Parachute and Glider Training School (P & GTS) and Horsa gliders were then added to the establishment. Noted aviation writer and pilot John Fricker recalled after basic training at Upper Heyford, being bussed with fellow rookies to Weston for his first jump from the balloon. *"Our jokes are slightly strained, and the nervous chatter slowly subsides as we drive into the airfield and confront the slack-eared balloon tugging at its moorings."* John went on to complete 13 months as a Parachute Jumping Instructor (PJI) with 1 PTS. The Kite Balloon used for parachute instruction was the Mk XI, which was similar in shape to, and evolved from the barrage balloon, and this type continued in service until they were disbanded in 1995.

John Cummings attended Course No. 231, which arrived at Upper Heyford on 12 December and departed on 21 January 1948. John was a Gunner and his course comprised of 11 officers and 116 other ranks. Following six days of ground training two 700 ft (213.36 m) jumps were made from a balloon at Weston, one from the door of the balloon car and another from the floor hatch. Then followed six different jumps from Dakotas, one each of split fours, sticks of four and sticks of 10 from 800 ft (244 m), fours with kit bags from 1000 ft (305 m), and a stick of eight with valises and a stick of four at night, both from 800 ft (244 m). John suffered an injury to his right elbow on his 1000 ft (305 m) jump with a kitbag and completed his training on the next course. No 231 course ended with an 89% completion with the remaining pupils having failed, refused to jump or injured.

Nurses make the high jump

During 1948 the powers that be thought it desirable to create a mobile force to drop, in emergencies, onto locations inaccessible to surface transport and as the helicopter was only in its infancy the parachute seemed the obvious medium to use. For immediate medical assistance at crashes an airborne medical team consisting of a medical officer, nursing sisters and medical orderlies were selected from volunteers from Princess Mary's RAF Nursing Service. The first team arrived at Upper Heyford on 20 September and underwent ground training, two descents from a balloon and then dropped by

Dakotas from 800 ft at Weston. Their seventh jump gave them a lifelike scenario when three casualties awaited them on the ground at Weston and the team was duly dropped, with kitbags of medical equipment, to tend the casualties; tents and other heavy equipment being dropped in containers. Four nursing sisters and a WAAF admin officer were in this first team and they became the first women ever to complete an RAF parachuting course. The second team underwent the four week training early in 1949 and at the time it was intended that there should be six courses a year but it is not known how many were completed prior to the task being taken over by the helicopter.

Kite balloon operations

Barrage balloons had been adapted for use by parachute training schools in 1941, leading to the development of the purpose built Mark IXD from which over the ensuing years many thousands of parachutists made their initial jumps. They are remembered with mixed feelings by those that jumped from them at Weston, and other locations, but this method remained on the airfield, with only a three year break, when they moved to Abingdon in the early fifties, for almost fifty years. It came into use as being the more economic option to utilising aircraft for the task but was very dependant on prevailing weather conditions. The hydrogen filled balloon was moored on an omni-directional balloon bed, which facilitated inflation, deflation and balloon servicing regardless of wind direction. The bed could be permanent, completely concreted with fixed anchorage points; semi-permanent, with anchorage points attached to concrete blocks sank into the ground; or temporary, for short duration balloon operations 'in the field,' using plates secured with pickets. Each had a central anchorage point and the whole was operated and controlled with flexible steel wire cables and strops. A 1947 aerial photo shows two permanent balloon beds positioned south of the technical site, and one remains today which from the air appears like a giant cartwheel. Semi-permanent and temporary beds have also been used on the airfield over the years.

Latterly the Balloon System comprised of the Mk XID Kite Balloon with a Mk 3 Balloon Car and

Above: Taken by a Benson based 82 Sqn aircraft on 16 April 1947 the airfield was still much as it was during the latter stages of the war. Two 1 PTS kite balloons can be seen, one on a permanent 'cartwheel' mooring, and another on a temporary base. All hangars remain in tact including the blister types to the north and south of the airfield. *(Author's collection)*

Left:This 1947 view shows a balloon moored alongside a short lived track running south from the technical site.
(Via John Norris)

associated airborne, mooring and inflation equipment and a truck mounted winch. The Balloon Car was a simple wooden structure, designed to carry an instructor and five pupils and was suspended from the balloon by a system of wire cables and exit was through a side door or a hatch in the floor, the latter method being later disbanded. The balloon remained moored to the bed until required for use when it was transferred to a winch and normally operated at 800 ft (244 m) although the maximum permitted height was 1500 ft (457 m).

Below: One of the RAF
nurses leaves a Dakota in
September 1948 *(1 PTS)*

USAF Packets

Parachute training was disrupted when the Dakotas were called on to take part in Operation 'Plainfare', the airlift of supplies to the beleaguered city of Berlin between mid-1948 and mid-1949. The Halifaxes had been withdrawn by this time but the USAF came to the rescue by periodically providing a Fairchild C-82 Packet, which was able to carry 42 paras, in return for the testing of the defences of their UK bases.

The *Oxford Times* for 7 April 1950 reported the breakaway of a balloon during gales on 31 March. The balloon had been close hauled and after it broke free it drifted over London causing reports of sightings of a "flying saucer." During the year Upper Heyford was taken over by the USAF as a bomber base and 1 P & GTS was eased out and settled at Abingdon, Berkshire as No. 1 Parachute School on 10 June with ten Dakota C4, six Horsa gliders and one Oxford, initially using Watchfield, Berks as its DZ, Weston having lost this task on 9 August. Weston was then taken over by the Air Positioning Plotting Unit and later placed in 'Care and Maintenance.' The role of 1 PTS was now to train Britain's airborne soldiers, providing basic static-line parachute training from both balloons and aircraft for the Regular and Territorial armies and on 1 November 1953 the School reverted to its 1 PTS title and Weston again became its DZ. The development of the parachutes used is always ongoing and the testing of all chutes and new equipment used by the paras are trialled by the Parachute Training School, in most cases at Weston.

Gliding returned in April when No. 130 Gliding

School moved in from Abingdon, equipped with elementary training gliders. Its role was to train Air Cadets and it remained on the airfield until disbanding on 1 September 1955. On 7 August 1954 local papers reported that 250 members of the 10th Battalion (TA) of the Parachute Regiment had jumped into Weston at dusk and delivered a night attack on the USAF at Upper Heyford.

Nurses of the first course attend lifelike casualties at Weston in September 1948 while members of the Press record the scene. *(1 PTS)*

In the early fifties sport parachuting became a regular part of air displays and a competitive sport and needless to say most successful jumpers were ex military trained paras and at around this time four ex PJIs formed the Apex Group and appeared at airshows around the country. In the first official World Parachuting Championships held at St Yan in France in 1954, the British team included five hastily trained 1 PTS PJIs, but alas they were outclassed.

Also in the early fifties 1 PTS Dakotas were replaced by Vickers Valettas, with a capacity for 20 paras, and the larger Handley Page Hastings, with a capacity for 32 paras, also came into use. In March 1956 47 Sqn. became the first unit to operate the Blackburn Beverly, which at the time was the largest aircraft to enter service with the RAF and able to carry 70 paratroops. For the next 11 years it was the workhorse in the training of paras for the RAF. 47 Sqn. formed a Flying Club and acquired Tiger Moth G-AOBH in May 1955 and over the next five years it was used for flying instruction and glider towing at Bicester and free-fall parachuting and glider towing at Weston.

Civilian gliding returns….

As was previously mentioned the Oxford Gliding Club (OGC) were in evidence at Weston in 1930 and later operated from Cumnor Meadow and Aston Rowant until the outbreak of war. It was not until 1951 that the club was reformed at Kidlington,

Another 1 PTS Dakota, KK138/S, drops at Weston. *(Via Mike Gibson)*

The Vickers Valetta took over from the Dakota with 1 PTS (1PTS)

where it remained until 1956 when it lost its accommodation and moved to Weston. In a letter from the club secretary dated 24 July 1956, members were told that the Club had permission to operate from Weston at weekends from 28 July and that gliding would cease whenever para drops take place. At this time the club operated at least EoN Olympia 2 BGA 515, Slingsby T21 Sedbergh BGA 700, a Kirby Cadet and a Grunau Baby. Permission was also given to aero tow and long time OGC member John Gibbons notes from his log book that he towed with Kidlington based Tiger Moth G-AOEL in July 1958 and later Oxford Aeroplane Club Tigers G-ALNA and G-AMEY were also hired for this purpose. John also recalls flying Miles Messenger G-AJFF, which was owned by an OGC member from Weston during 1957 and 1958.

...and para clubs form

During 1956 the Abingdon Parachute Club was formed at the instigation of Sgt J N Hoffman and jumps were made at Weston from the 47 Sqn. Flying Club Tiger which was normally flown by Master Pilot Jerry Schellong who would later fly Rapides from the airfield. A para was carried in the front seat and when it was time to jump the pilot would tap him on the shoulder, he would then step out onto the starboard wing, facing the pilot, and when the pilot nodded he would let go and count to three before pulling the rip cord. On 23 April 1957 Hoffman set an unofficial delayed-drop record of 41 seconds when he jumped from the Tiger at 8400ft (2560 m) and fell to around 2000 ft (609.6 m) before opening his chute. Using the same mount, in the summer Flt.Lt. Neil Perry dropped from 2500 ft (762 m) and made a ten second delayed drop but sadly, during a jump in July, his chute failed to open and he was killed and this led to the closure of the Club. Peter Hearn in his book 'Falcons – Men who train the Paras' quotes the PTS motto 'Knowledge Dispels Fear' and states that nowhere is this more apt than in free fall.

Pilots from nearby Upper Heyford whose normal mounts were Boeing B-47 bombers based

The Beverley was in service from 1956 until 1968 (1 PTS)

their USAF Aero Club Piper J3C-65 Cub N30744 for a time before transferring it to Greenham Common, Berks in April 1957. In November Whirlwind helicopters were used to fly in troops from RAF Abingdon during an exercise with the Territorials.

Free fall sport parachuting was now a worldwide sport and the French military, in particular, were keen participants, so much so and not to be left behind in the latest developments, 1 PTS sent four PJIs to the French Military Parachute School at Pau for free fall training in 1959, and possibly in connection with this, during September jumps were made at Weston from a French Air Force Noratlas.

Some jumps were made from a USAF Fairchild C-119 Packet in May 1959, and Twin Pioneers were being used during July and August when 142 day and 21 night jumps were recorded, 16 day jumps

The Hastings was operated in the para role from the early fifties until1967 (1 PTS)

Aerial view mid fifties. *(Via John Norris)*

also being undertaken from an unidentified Helicopter. September must have set a record for 1 PTS as 2456 jumps were recorded, 143 from balloons, 552 day and 120 night from Hastings and 1419 day and 222 night from Beverleys. A French Air Force Noratlas was seen again on 7 September when 1 PTS trialled French parachutes.

An article in *Flight* for 6 May 1960 looked at the training involved to become a para in the Army. It detailed the training given at Aldershot, the HQ of the Parachute Regiment, and with 1 PTS at Abingdon with initial jumps from static balloons leading to drops from aircraft at their Weston DZ. The aircraft used at the time were Abingdon based 47 and 53 Sqn Beverleys and Hastings from RAF Colerne, Wiltshire. At the time 1 PTS had about 300 trainees manning two Regular Army and two Territorial Army (TA) four week courses. On the course eight training jumps were made, the initial two from a static balloon at 800 ft (243.8 m) followed by six from aircraft, including two with a weapon container and one at night (the TA did not do night jumps). The jumps at Weston were made up of (1) in consecutive sticks of three, (2) simultaneous sticks of three, (3) simultaneous sticks of ten, (4) with equipment in sticks of five, (5) by night and (6) en-masse with 40 to 60 troops deplaning at a time.

The expertise developed by 1 PTS PJIs led to the formation of the RAF Parachute Display Team in 1961. The team undertook weekend displays in addition to their training and trials work during weekdays, both in the UK and Europe and also taking part in competitions world wide. A pit was dug in the centre of the airfield and filled with pea sand as a touch down point when practicing for competition work and this is still very much in evidence and can be seen for miles and is a useful location aid for paras today.

The Armstrong Whitworth Argosy entered squadron service as a medium range tactical transport at nearby RAF Benson in February 1962 and with a capacity for 54 paratroops was soon put into use by 1 PTS. Other than the normal jump platforms, 67 jumps were made from a Twin Pioneer in July and the following month 24 from a Beaver and 101 from Dakotas during August and September. During the year the RAF Abingdon

Above: Oxford Gliding Club members making the best of the autumn sun on 13 October 1956 with Olympia and Grunu Baby waiting at the launch point.

Left: Another Oxford Gliding Club member receives a briefing from his instructor in a T21BBGA 700 on 13 October 1956. This glider sadly stalled and crashed with two fatalities in 1967.
(both John Bolt)

Sport Parachuting Club was formed and two ex-Fleet Air Arm DH 89 Dominies, were acquired from RNAS Lossiemouth for a princely sum of £400, which included two spare engines, and were registered G-ASFC and G-ASIA. Only G-ASFC was civilianised and made its first drops at Weston on 28 August 1963 but by mid-65 it was withdrawn and stored until the fuselage was converted to a ground trainer in January 1967 and the wings were burnt

John Gibbons aero-towed with Tiger Moth G-AODX, loaned from the CFS Little Rissington Flying Club, between August 1960 and September 1961, Beagle Terrier G-ASBU between October 1962 and June 1965 and Piper Super Cub G-AREU during June

This 1957 photo has it all, OGC T-21, balloon and buildings including water tower, hangar and watch office. (
via Norman Woodward)

Traces of the wartime hedge-row camouflage are still visible in this 1956 view but the track seen in 1947 has gone
(Author's collection)

and July 1963. During the mid-sixties Auster J/1N G-AIBZ was purchased by a group of Club members and was in use until 1969 when the RAF withdrew permission to aero tow.

Bristol Fighters resurface

The Bristol F2B fuselage frames which had been acquired from the airfield by Mr Boddington in 1919 came to light in the mid-sixties when six were found to be supporting the roof of a barn/workshop. They were recovered by the RAF Museum who used one in the restoration of a static exhibit and disposed of the rest. The current status of this important cache is:

(1) Royal Air Force Museum, Hendon: Carries serial E2466 – static exhibit

(2) Aero Vintage, Old Warden, Beds: Registered as G-AANM in 1987 with serial D7889 - airworthy.

(3) Patina Ltd operated by The Fighter Collection, Duxford, Cambs: Rebuilt as a composite also using parts from F4516. Registered as G-ACAA in 1991 with serial D8084 - airworthy

(4) Royal Army and Military History Museum, Brussels, Belgium: Rebuilt as a composite using some parts from J8264 - static exhibit with serial B4

(5) Peter R Jackson, Omaka, New Zealand: Under restoration as D8084

(6) Vintage Aviation Heritage Foundation, Old Kingsbury Aerodrome, Seguin, Texas, USA: Under restoration

One of the Bristol Fighter fuselage frames seen supporting the workshop roof in 1960. *(via Mike Gibson)*

Interesting view of Weston circa 1958/59 with Twin Pioneer taking off with three storey watch office behind T2 hangar. *(Carrick Watson)*

Hastings tragedy – the RAF's worst accident to date

A tragic accident occurred at 4 pm on 6 July 1963 when Colerne based 36 Sqn. Handley Page Hastings C1 TG577 had just taken off from Abingdon, with a crew of five and 38 RAF and Army parachutists, bound for the DZ at Weston when the crew reported 'sloppy controls' and requested a priority landing. The Hastings did not, however, reach Abingdon but crashed with the loss of all lives near Dorchester on Thames. The accident, in terms of fatalities, was the worst ever suffered by the RAF and was attributed to metal fatigue of two elevator bolts causing additional stress to two more bolts which also failed.

Another Rapide and birth of the Falcons display team

Seven para descents were made from a Beaver during January 1964 and 128 during August and September from a Handley Page Herald in connection with clearance trials and it is assumed that this was for the Royal Malaysian Air Force that operated eight of the type. Rapide G-AGSH was acquired by RAF (Abingdon) Sport Parachute Association in May 1965 and was soon in service dropping paras at Weston, a task it was to fulfil for some 20 years. The Hawker Siddeley Andover began operating from Abingdon in December 1966 and although smaller than the Argosy, was able to carry 30 paratroops and was soon seen at Weston.

Possibly taken in the fifties; the NAAFFI wagon was essential for the well being of the troops. *(Via John Norris)*

Right: John Gibbons poses by Oxford Aero Club Tiger Moth G-ALNA which he borrowed on occasions to aero tow OGC gliders. (via John Gibbons)

Below: A Kite Balloon at its mooring getting the full effect of gusty conditions. Romney Sheds and water tower are seen in the background.
(John Lawrence)

Gliding Club fatalities and C-130 Hercules enters service

On 9 April 1967 Slingsby T21B, BGA 700, of the OGC stalled at a height from which recovery was impossible and crashed with loss of the instructor and pupil. The incident happened during an approach to land in turbulent wind conditions when the glider suddenly pitched into a dive from about 150 ft (45.7 m). The club was in need of modern equipment and two Schleicher ASK-13 gliders were acquired new, CCE later in the year and CGQ in 1969.

During August 1967 another new type, the Lockheed C-130 Hercules entered service with the RAF, becoming the services standard medium range transport, operating out of RAF Lyneham in Wiltshire, a role it still undertakes today, operating from the same base. Able to drop 64 paratroops in one stick, the Hercules was soon

The RAF Parachute Display Team which had been operating as such since 1961 was now an established integral part of the School and during the year was officially named 'The Falcons'. It now received funding for the training and running of an officially recognised team. Recorded jumps made during December were 112 from Balloons, 329 day and 41 night from Hastings, 111 day and 4 night from Beverleys and 37 night from an Argosy.

The author accompanied Brantly B2B G-ASEH from Kidlington on 12 March 1964 to carry out general maintenance duties when it flew a BBC cameraman filming paras jumping from Rapide G-ASFC. *(Author)*

Above: Rapide G-ASFC was only in use for two years before being withdrawn in 1965.*(Author's collection)*

Right:Auster J/1N G-AIBZ was purchased by a group of OGC members and was in use by the club for aero tows in the mid-sixties. *(John Gibbons)*

seen disgorging its load over Weston, replacing the Hastings in this role when it retired during the year and the Beverley which survived for another year. Over the years the Hercules has proved to be the most suitable military jump platform ever.

A landmark was reached in the history of 1 PTS when on 6 March 1969 18 year old Private Blunn made his first jump from an aircraft which was also the unit's one millionth descent when he jumped from a 30 Sqn Hercules on to the Weston DZ.

Hot air sojourns ...

The British Balloon and Airship Club (BBAC) was inaugurated in 1965 and an early member, Wg. Cdr. Gerry Turnbull of 1 PTS, instigated the formation of the RAF Free Balloon Club the following year. An imported American hot air balloon, known as the "Red Monster" underwent flight trials at Weston in 1966, in the hands of Turnbull and Flt Lt Stuart Cameron. An early British design the Thorn K-800 Coal Gas Balloon G-ATGN was damaged during the August and this also ended up at Weston for repairs and improvements. The January 1967 *BBAC Newsletter* noted that at Weston; *"Hot air balloon flights, as opposed to experimental hops across the*

airfield, now take place on suitable Wednesday afternoons." No doubt an enjoyable pursuit on the traditional service sports afternoon!

A BBAC meeting was held at Weston on 16 August when the guest speaker was American

Below: The Hot-Air Group's Bristol Belle G-AVTL made its first controlled free flight rom Weston on 9 August 1967 *(Author's collection)*

Above: In this April 1966 aerial two kite balloons are moored, the newer permanent mooring below the 'cartwheel' was added in the early fifties.   Left: A very nervous pupil making one of his early descents from a Kite Balloon. *(Author's collection)*
Below: Twin Pioneers were one of the more unusual types used in the sixties. *(Via W J Busbell)*

balloonist Don Piccard. Blustery wind conditions kept visiting balloons earthbound although Piccard made a "fast drag" across the airfield. Brighton AX7-65 hot air balloon "Bristol Belle" tore itself apart on its initial inflation in June 1967 and after a rebuild by the Hot-Air Group as their _ Free Balloon it was registered as G-AVTL. Turnbull agreed to help the Group to fly it at Weston and he made its first flight across the airfield on 9 July witnessed by a team from the *Daily Telegraph* colour supplement. Crewed by Mark Westwood and Don Cameron with Turnbull supervising it made the first controlled free flight by a modern British built hot air balloon from Weston on 9 August, landing at RAF Bicester. More

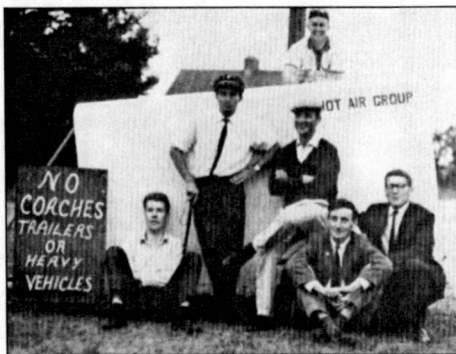

A happy Hot-Air Group pose in the village in 1968
(Author's collection)

flights were made from Weston and on 7 July 1968 it was noted as making the short hop from the gates of Blenheim Palace to the airfield. An unregistered Western 20 hot air balloon made its maiden flight from the airfield in the hands of messrs Turnbull, Westwood and Bulmer on the 20th May 1970, and subsequently became G-AYMV. As a postscript Gerry Turnbull and Mark Westwood formed Western Balloons and Don Cameron went on to form Cameron Balloons. In 1967 the RAF (Abingdon) Sport Parachuting Club was renamed the RAF Sport Parachuting Association (RAFSPA) with the aim to bring sport parachuting within the reach of all members of the RAF. Shortly after its own display team the 'Robins' was formed to perform at events in the south of England, jumping from the associations Rapide G-AGSH. Most of the team members were ex Falcons and the name was later more appropriately changed to "The Hawks Parachute Display Team."

. . and return to parachuting

Edward Cartner, a PJI with 1 PTS, recalled that by 1968 at the end of his first tour there were at least two married quarters at Weston "...glorified Secco huts, realy" where the Flt.Lt. C.O. and a Wt.Off., both PJIs, were accommodated. He returned to 1 PTS in 1972 and believes that the Watch Office was demolished at around this time and replaced by a redundant runway control caravan. Although only intended as a temporary measure, this was still going strong in 1984! Edward also recalled that "...*for many years around the late 1970s*

Above: Rapide G-AGSH was in service at Weston from 1965 until 1975. *(Author's collection)*

Left: Sgt PJIs Bob Kent, Ray Willis and Bob Souter pose with G-AGSH in 1970. (Bob Norris)

Above: The Watch Office which was built in 1942 was demolished in the early seventies. *(Brian Martin/ARG Collection)*

Left:Cessna 210D G-ASWO saw use by RAFSPA during the seventies and is seen here sans door at Kidlington. *(Author)*

Below: Twin Otter G-BFGP was first seen in September 1990. *(Mike Gibson)*

accommodation was provided by old style QRA caravans that were positioned opposite the guardroom and mess hall. Similarly, the cookhouse and catering arrangements were greatly improved in the late 1970s (I think) and that made a great difference for those who frequently spent a full day at Weston." The caravans were actually around twenty old railway carriages which were donated by a generous civilian benefactor who had made a jump there.

The *Oxford Mail* for 11 March 1968 noted that 20 aircraft had left Abingdon for Weston the previous day carrying from six to fifteen paras and that a Private in the TA had died after jumping from an Argosy. An unusual glider used by the OGC in the early seventies was the Hawkridge Kittiwake, which was a Slingsby T.15 Gull 3 rebuilt by the Hawkridge Aircraft Co post war. By the late sixties Beagle Husky G-ATCD, which was based on a strip at nearby Middleton Stoney, was undertaking aerotows and in May 1970 it was registered to The

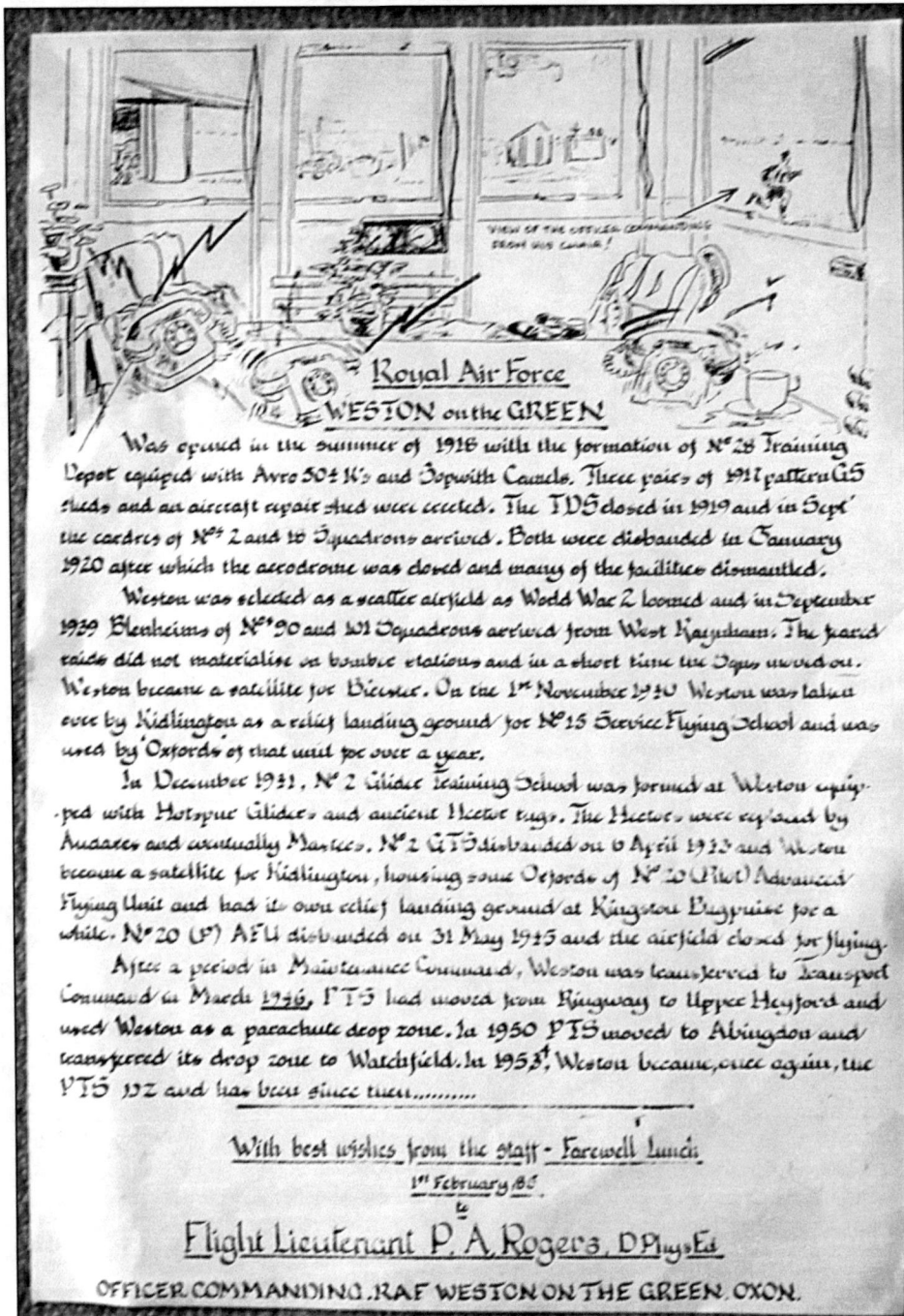

Royal Air Force
WESTON on the GREEN

Was opened in the summer of 1918 with the formation of N° 28 Training Depot equiped with Avro 504 K's and Sopwith Camels. Three pairs of 1917 pattern GS sheds and an aircraft repair shed were erected. The TDS closed in 1919 and in Sept' the cadres of N°s 2 and 10 Squadrons arrived. Both were disbanded in January 1920 after which the aerodrome was closed and many of the facilities dismantled.

Weston was selected as a scatter airfield as World War 2 loomed and in September 1939 Blenheims of N° 90 and 101 Squadrons arrived from West Raynham. The feared raids did not materialise on bomber stations and in a short time the Sqns moved on. Weston became a satellite for Bicester. On the 1st November 1940 Weston was taken over by Kidlington as a relief landing ground for N° 15 Service Flying School and was used by Oxfords of that unit for over a year.

In December 1941, N° 2 Glider Training School was formed at Weston equipped with Hotspur Gliders and ancient Hector tugs. The Hectors were replaced by Audaxes and eventually Masters. N° 2 GTS disbanded on 6 April 1943 and Weston became a satellite for Kidlington, housing some Oxfords of N° 20 (Pilot) Advanced Flying Unit and had its own relief landing ground at Kingston Bagpuize for a while. N° 20 (P) AFU disbanded on 31 May 1945 and the airfield closed for flying.

After a period in Maintenance Command, Weston was transferred to Transport Command in March 1946, PTS had moved from Ringway to Upper Heyford and used Weston as a parachute drop zone. In 1950 PTS moved to Abingdon and transferred its drop zone to Watchfield. In 1953, Weston became, once again, the PTS DZ and has been since then..........

With best wishes from the staff - Farewell Lunch
1st February 185
to
Flight Lieutenant P. A. Rogers, DPhysEd
OFFICER COMMANDING, RAF WESTON ON THE GREEN, OXON.

Brief history of station presented to Flt. Lt. P A Rogers O.C. Weston at his farewell lunch on 1 February 1985. *(Via Mike Westwood)*

Oxford Flying and Gliding Group. 'TCD remained in use until the early eighties when the strip closed and it relocated to Enstone and since then there have only been occasional aerotows, with special permission, using tug aircraft from local gliding sites. John Norris recalls that GQ Parachutes positioned a Skyvan at Weston in November 1971 for filming jumps from 12, 000 ft (3657.6 m) with the new Dominator canopy, which took place over two weekends. He later jumped from a Cessna 172 on 13 February 1972 and a Cessna 182 on 1 April, the identities of which were not recorded and around this time a Cessna 180 was loaned from Netheravon as was their Rapide G-AGTM.

The Argosy had been the mount for the Falcons for some years but in 1970 this role was taken over by RAF Lyneham based C-130 Hercules. During the seventies the Tri-Service Adventure Training Scheme trained free fall parachuting at Weston under the auspices of PTS, to promote "military qualities" in its pupils. With the run down of Bicester and the relocation of 71 Maintenance Unit to Abingdon the Belfast Servicing Flight and the Joint Air Transport Evaluation Unit moved to Brize Norton in 1975 followed by 1 PTS in January 1976. Again, this new base was still within easy reach of Weston and it continued as the DZ. Bryan Morris became OC Weston in August 1976 when the permanent staff comprised, himself, a Station Warrant Officer, a Sgt PJI, a Cpl clerk and two cooks. Additionally, the Adventurous Training Flight had its OC, a Flt. Ggt and four Sgt PJIs and the balloon unit had a Sgt and a Cpl and a dozen or so MT drivers, which were withdrawn the following year to their parent unit RAF Hullavington. Thereafter balloons were provided as and when required by a mobile balloon unit.

At some stage, possibly in the sixties, Rapide G-ASIA also found its way to Weston, its remains and those of the G-ASFC surviving until the late seventies when they were burnt. Long serving Rapide G-AGSH was sold in 1975 when RAFSPA acquired Cessna U206 G-ASVN which remained in use for five years until it was replaced with TU206G G-SKYE which was delivered on 23 January 1980 and remained in use for 23 years. Another Cessna, 210D G-ASWO, was used on occasions during the late seventies and G-AZRZ, a U206F, was hired from the Army Parachute Assn. during the '80s. Larger than the 206, a 207 was used

for a couple of years in the late seventies and was more popular, having a double door aperture. RAFSPA took charge of its own Islander when G-DIVE was registered to the RAF Parachute Assn at Weston in June 1978 (serial ZA503 was allocated but not used) and this was to remain in service until 1984. Twin Otter G-BKBC was on hire by RAFSPA in December 1982.

New Turbo Islander G-WOTG

Piston Islander G-DIVE was replaced with the new turbine powered 2T variant, appropriately registered G-WOTG, which was collected new from the factory on the Isle of Wight on 27 February 1984. For its dedicated role this was the first Islander to have a sliding cabin door fitted and was to serve the RAFSPA well for 21 years. Originally purchased by the MoD for a military role, which was subsequently cancelled, it was allocated the serial ZF444, but this was never carried and it first flew as G-BJYT and was re-registered as G-WOTG when the MoD allocated it to RAFSPA and the JSPC at Weston.

'Blue Peter' presenter John Noakes jumped with The Falcons in the 70s and in the succeeding years other presenters have followed his lead, co-presenter Janet Ellis joined team in 1984 and made a jump from a balloon, unfortunately breaking her hip in the process but returned later in the season to make a successful jump from a Hercules. A new aircraft type used in August 1985 when Short Skyvan G-OVAN was

Complete with 'Blue Peter Badge' on his helment, John Noakes prepared to jump with the Falcons. *(Simon Peters Collection)*

hired from the Peterborough Parachute Centre and piston engined powered Islander G-AXXJ put in appearances between July 1989 and May 1990 and then handed over to another of the type, G-AYRU, which came from the Joint Service Parachute Centre at Netheravon and was to be seen on various occasions until April 2003. Islander G-BENF was used for a time during May 1990 as was Skyvan G-BKMD from the London Parachute Centre at Cranfield and was to be seen at the airfield on various occasions until September 1991.

The Joint Services Adventurous Training Centre at Weston, staffed by PJIs from the 1 PTS Adventurous Training Flight ran two week, Monday to Friday, adventurous training sports parachute courses for beginners and advanced students. During 1990 eight basic courses trained 252 students, and three advanced courses trained a further 65, who made 800 freefall descents. There were excellent clubhouse facilities, including a nine-hole pitch and putt course, making it one of the leading parachute centres in the country. During the year the 1 PTS Military Training Flight also completed 30 courses, ranging from weekend to two weeks in duration, training personnel from the three services, around 1200 receiving their coveted wings and another eight were trained as PJIs going on to instruct with the PTS.

New hangar and operations building and largest aircraft visits

It is not often that one can report on the erection a new hangar but with assistance from the Sports Council the OGC had one built in the mid eighties and this was officially opened in 1986 by Douglas Hurd MP, who was the honorary President of the Club at that time. Up until this time the club had used the northern half of the T2 hangar and this was then refurbished and became the packing and training facility for RAFSPA and the JSPC. The OGC had added new aircraft during the eighties, two single-seat Schleicher Ka 8Bs CYZ and DSD, a high performance single-seat Grob G-102 Astir DMH and a 1952 vintage Slingsby T21B FGB came from an RAF auction. Ka 8B DSD survived around five years before being written off in a take-off accident on 2 January 1990 and was later replaced by another of the type, HFW.

Twin Otter G-BFGP was in use during September 1990 and in April 1991 Cessna U206E G-BSMB was hired from the Army Parachute Association and made many visits until August 1993 when their turbine Islander G-LEAP came into use and was to visit Weston

Above: The original T2 hangar was sectioned to provide a packing and training facility for RAFSPA after the OGS new hangar opened in 1986. *(Author)*

Above: Skyvan G-BKMD on hire from the London Skydiving Centre at Cranfield takes on fuel on 6 May 1990. *(Mike Gibson)*

Right: The OGC hangar which was opened by Douglas Hurd in 1986. *(Author)*

A pair of Wokkas!

Left: Chinook HC1 ZA682/BN from 18 Sqn, Gutersloh seen on 26 September 1991.

Below: 7 Sqn, Odiham Chinook HC1 ZA712/ER visited on 2 August 1991 *(both Mike Gibson)*

until May 2003. Military helicopters occasionally put in appearances, 7 Sqn Chinook ZA712/ER being noted on August 1991 and another of the type ZA682/BN from 18 Sqn the following month.

In remembrance of the Airborne Forces in Palestine,1945 – 1948, on 28 September 1992 commemorative covers were parachuted onto Weston DZ from a drop height of 1200 ft (366 m) with Cpl Jimmy Doig of 1 PTS from a 47 Sqn Hercules. A new operations building with an observation dome was built south of the T2 hangar and came into use in November 1993, for use when 1 PTS were dropping.

Turbine Islander, G-ORED, the mount of the Army Parachute Display Team, The Red Devils put in appearances between May 1993 and November 2002. 60 Sqn Wessex HC 2 from nearby Benson was in use on 19 April 1994 and the largest aircraft ever to have had any involvement with Weston was USAF Lockheed C-5B Galaxy 87-0033 of the 436th Airlift Wing from Dover AFB, Delaware which dropped 1 PTS paras during the early evening of 2 September. Needless to say, this event having the effect of an eclipse caused some consternation in the village as it was assumed that it was having difficulties. The Galaxy had earlier taken off from Upper Heyford.

Eastern bloc aircraft

With the demise of the Berlin Wall in 1989 many aircraft from former Eastern Block countries made their way to parachuting centres across Europe, the Let 410 twin turboprop being the most popular. The first such aircraft to reach Weston was Hungarian registered Antanov An-28 HA-LAJ, which was on lease with two Russian pilots from 27 August until 6 September 1993. It arrived late in the afternoon of the 27th and the following day, having already completed 12 flights of around 15 minute duration with up to 17 parachutists, on the 13th with another lift of 17 and two crew as it reached 500 ft (152.4

C-5B Galaxy 87-0033 makes low pass over the airfield after disgorging a 1 PTS team on 2 September 1994 *(Mike Gibson)*

Whoops!

An-28 HA-LAJ
returning from
another drop on 28
August 1993. it was
soon to come to an
unfortunate demise.
(Mike Gibson)

HA-LAJ at rest, while a
former 'occupant' looks
on
(Author's collection)

HA-LAJ where it came to
rest in a field across the
Chesterton road on 28
August.
(Author's collection)

Some of the jumpers
pose after their lucky
escape with the ill fated
HA-LAJ.
(Author's collection)

The new Operations building with a glass dome came into use in November 1993. *(Author)*

m) both engines simultaneously suffered a total power loss when both propellers auto-feathered due to an electrical defect. Take off had been on Runway 36 and a forced landing was made in a field of cut crop to the north of the airfield across the Chesterton road. The landing was heavy causing the aircraft to be a write-off but fortunately all occupants walked from the scene uninjured. Harking back to earlier days, Battle of Britain Flight Dakota ZA947 was used by 1 PTS on 21 March 1994 possibly in connection with a commemorative event. Ukranian registered Let 410UVP, UR-67477, was hired in May 1994 and from May until June Islander G-BJSA was also used. The workhorse of the Soviet-bloc parachuting scene for so many years, the indomitable Antanov An-2 biplane, only appears to have made brief appearances; the first noted being UK based Slovac registered OM-UIN in June.

After half a century Kite Balloons make last deflation

RAF balloon operations were disbanded on 30 March 1995, bringing to a close almost five decades of this familiar sight on the Weston skyline when the kite balloons were withdrawn from service and seen no more. As a cost-cutting exercise their role had been contracted out to Hunting Aviation to provide any MoD paratroop training with two Short Skyvans operating out of Oxford Airport. During this transition period an all white 7 Sqn Chinook ZA682 was noted during May and 18 Sqn Puma XW236 in June. The first Hunting Aviation Skyvan to be seen was Luxemburg registered LX-JUL which was in use

Roundels were not normally applied to Kite Balloons so this October 1994 shot is rather unusual *(Mike Gibson)*

Compared with the 1947 aerial this shot taken in June 1994, the perimeter track and apart from the T2 all wartime hangars have now disappeared. Above and to the right of the T2 are caravans, the new OGC hangar and numerous glider trailers.
(Author's collection)

by May and in December it was appropriately registered as G-PIGY, and is still hired in 2007, albeit with a new owner. The second, G-BVXW, was used from mid-1996 until 2004.

Another Turbine Islander came on the scene with RAFSPA in May 1995 with the arrival of G-PASU and this was hired on occasions until April 2000 and in October Skyvan LX-DEF was making

drops. Boscombe Down based Harvard KF183 was used as a camera ship filming exits from the Hunting Skyvans during July 1996.

During August RAFSPA hired three hot air balloons when two carried three parachutists and the third eight.

Above: Slovac registered An-2 OM-UIN at rest in June 1994

Left: The first Czech built Let 410 to be used at Weston was Ukranian registered UR-67477 seen on approach on 1 May 1994.
(both Mike Gibson)

ISLANDERS AND 'VANS AT WESTON

Above: Islander G-BJSA being refuelled at Weston on 29 May 1994 was on hire for that years summer season. *(Author)*

Right: Turbine Islander G-PASU seen coming in to land on 6 May 1995 was a regular visitor until April 2000.
(Mike Gibson)

Skyvan LX-DEF returning from another sortie on 22 October 1995. (Mike Gibson)

Above: Skyvans G-BVXW and G-PIGY await their next 1 PTS sorties in April 1996.
(Mike Gibson)

Right: Hunting Skyvan LX-JUL was registered G-PIGY in December 1995 and is seen in September 1998 in full Hunting livery and titles.
(Mike Gibson)

Left: all-white painted7 Sqn Chinook HC 2 ZA682 at rest on 5 May 1995. From the oil-streaks around the engine, it looks as if it's had a problem! *(Mike Gibson)*

BelowPuma HC1 XW236 was used on 14 June 1995 *(Mike Gibson)*

When they jumped, the DZ was missed and they landed at Wendlebury, damaging power lines and causing a blackout in the village, one jumper gaining the name "Sparky" after the incident. Another balloon was used to scatter the ashes of a skydiver.

Czech registered Let 410UVP OK-NDG was hired in August 1998 and another of the type, Hungarian registered HA-LAY, in July 1999. Dornier Do 28D-2 Skyservant G-BWCN put in an appearance in June 1999 and two turbo Islanders were hired in August, The Rhine Army Parachute Association providing G-JSAT and Police Aviation Services G-PASV. Danish registered Turbo Beaver OY-JRR Black Beaver was first seen in 2000 and made many more visits and Swiss Twin Otter HB-LTG was based for the 2001 March to October season. In 2000 the pilot of Black Beaver brought Hungarian registered Antanov An-2, HA-ABP, from Hinton-in-the-Hedges and some RAFSPA members took the opportunity to jump from it before it departed to its base and they were also able to add another type when Cessna Caravan G-EELS was hired for a weekend during the summer.

More accidents and a new mount for RAFSPA

A soldier died in January 2000 after cutting away his main canopy and attempting to open his reserve too close to the ground after jumping from a Hercules.

Above: Piston powered Dornier 28D-2 G-BWCN was the first of the type to be noted at Weston and is seen on 5 June 1999. It was re-engined and returned as HA-ACO in June 2003

Left: Let 410 OK-NDG put in an appearance in August 1998. *(both Mike Gibson)*

Right: RAFSPA Cessna TU 206G G-SKYE was a Weston resident for 24 years and is seen at rest on 18 June 2000. (Author)

Below: Another Let 410 HA-LAY was hired in July 1999. (MiKe Gibson)

Helicopters were not a common sight at Weston but Fleet Air Arm Sea King HC 4 ZF119/VW of 846 Sqn was noted disgorging troops on 7 June 2001. Danish Nomad OY-JRW was hired in April 2002 but crashed into the bomb store on the north side of the field on the 13th after an aborted take off. The two pilots were unscathed but several of the 12 parachutists on board were not so fortunate and sustained injuries. To prevent a reoccurrence the bomb store and nearby air raid shelter were raised to the ground. Another Caravan, PH-JAS, was hired

in the July. There was another fatality on Easter weekend 2003 when a RAFSPA member was caught by a freak gust of wind just prior to landing and was sent tumbling to the ground. Former air mapping Let 410 HA-YFC which had a glazed nose was in service during March and another unusual type hired initially during the year was the single engined Russian built SMG 92 Turbo Finist HA-YDF which was similar in appearance to the Beaver and this was to put in more appearances until August 2005. A type first used in 1999 which became the mainstay with RAFSPA until the present day is the German build Dornier 28G92 Turbo Skyservant twin which has a capacity for 15 paras in comparison to the Islanders 10 and has a faster climb to altitude. The first dedicated RAFSPA aircraft was Hungarian registered, HA-ACL, which was hired in April 2003, and this ex Luftwaffe machine was joined by another of the type, HA-ACO in June. 'CO was not new to Weston as it had put in an appearance two years earlier

Above: A single load of RAFSPA members were able to add An-2 HA-ABP to their log books during 2000. (Author)

Right: Danish Turbo Beaver "Black Beaver" returns from a drop in June 2000.(Author)

TWOTTERS, 'SERVANTS AND PARACHUTES!

Above: Turbo Skyservant HA-ACO was the more colourful of the two with its two-tone blue and white scheme and has been hired-in many times since 2003. *(Author)*

Left: The Falcons during a practice jump from 33 Sqn Puma XW223 on 19 August 1998 *(Mike Gibson)*

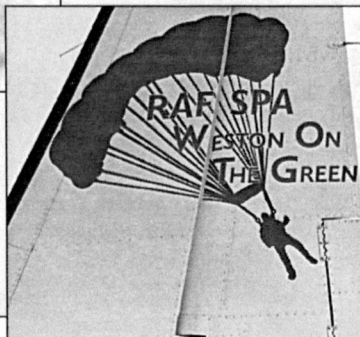

CAUTION
PARACHUTE DROP ZONE
PARACHUTING IN PROGRESS

Above: The motif on G-WOTG's fin and also on that on G-SKYE leaves no doubt of the aircrafts ownership. *(Author)*

Still wearing the camouflage from its Luftwaffe past Turbo Skyservant HA-ACL returns for another load in June 2003 *(Author)*

Right: Pleasing shot of Twin Otter HB-LTG coming into land in May 2001 with OGC K13 in background. *(Mike Gibson)*

Right: Danish registered Nomad OY-JRW came to grief after it hit an air raid shelter after aborting take off on 13 April 2002. *(Author)*

Below: The sign on Weston's gate with crests of 1 PTS, Joint Services Parachute Centre, RAFSPA and Falcons Display Team. *(Author)*

as G-BWCN, then piston powered. In August 2004 Islander G-AXZK was hired from nearby Hinton-in-the-Hedges and during the year the guards who manned the main gate and were provided by RAF Brize Norton were dispensed with and the guardroom became a gymnasium.

owner in Scotland. It was delivered to Cumbernauld Airport on 22 April 2005 by weekend volunteer Ray Evans who had collected the aircraft new from the factory in 1984 accompanied by Weston's chief pilot Mike Westwood, leaving Dornier 28 HA-ACL as the sole occupant. It wasn't to be the last time it would be seen at Weston as it returned in July to help with the busy summer season, returning to Scotland on 19 August.

Also in April, LET 410 HA-YFC arrived from South Cerney for a two month stay, handing over to another of the type HA-LAQ from Hinton in May and Lindstrand hot air balloon G-BUZJ launched from the field on 7 June. Sporting paras like to jump from different aircraft types and this was the reason for Agusta 109 G-TELY and Jet Ranger G-BTHY helicopters being used in August and September

Departure of long serving G-WOTG

Turbine Islander G-WOTG, an aircraft which had introduced thousands to skydiving at Weston during more than 22,000 sorties over its 21 year tenure was sold to a new

Long serving G-WOTG was sold to a new owner in 2005 (Author's collection)

Above: Bicester based Oxford University Gliding Club Grob Astir CS FEF took part in the Nationals at Weston on 2 September 2000 *(Author)*

Left: Oxford Gliding Club ASK 13 CGQ waiting to launch on 29 March 2002 *(Author)*

Right: OGC's Glaser-Dirks Orion JSX at rest on 29 March 2002 *(Author)*

SILENT FLIGHT AT WESTON

Above: Oxford Gliding Club fleet at rest in July 2001. *(Author)*

Left: Oxford University Gliding Club T.21 FGB seen in the OGC hangar on 17 July 1999. *(Author)*

Dutch Cessna Caravan PH-JAS has put in many appearances since July 2002. (Mike Gibson)

came into being on 1 March 2006. Facilities at this time included a new clubhouse and gear store, the packing hangar and creeping facilities, a camping ground and the same coaches and training staff. The civilian management for this new venture are each

and during September and October another Dornier Turbo Skyservant, HA-VOC, was in use and has seen regular use since when HA-ACL has been away for maintenance. The Army brought in there latest attack helicopter on 11 October when Apache AH1 ZJ182 visited on a training flight from Wattisham.

long time RAFSPA jumpers. Weston is now widely regarded as the best jumping area in the UK and the training provided can equal the best in Europe. Skydive Weston achieved notoriety in August 2006 when their all female Team Airkix won the World Championships for Freestyle and Artistics at Gera, Germany.

Another Turbo Finist was seen on 5 May 2007 when HA-NAH made its first visit when on hire to Skydive Weston and by August they were using Skyvan G-PIGY. Skydive Weston and RAFSPA are now operating as a single entity with the latter, without assets, surviving in name only to look after

Skydive Weston, the latest resident

RAFSPA was run as a secondary duty by personnel from RAF Brize Norton but latterly they were non-volunteers, and not always weekend skydivers, and as operational commitments meant that they had less spare time it was decided to hand over responsibility for weekend parachuting at Weston to a civilian organisation. Hence the formation of Skydive Weston Ltd, a skydiving school which

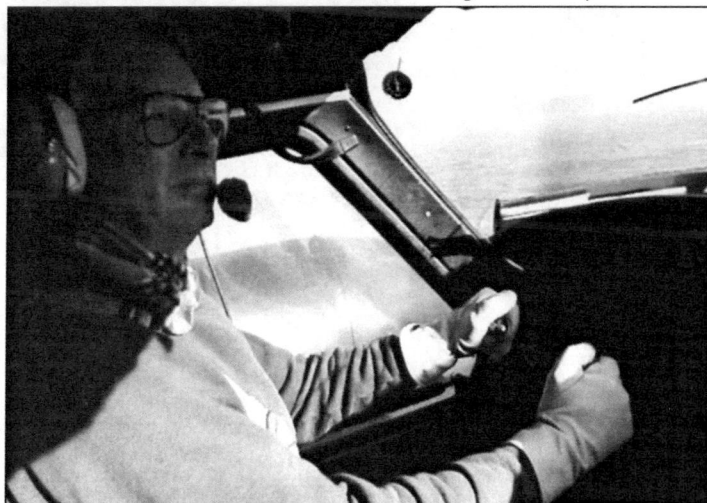

RAFSPA Chief Pilot Mike Westwood in his "office" Dornier 28 HA-ACL in October 2006. (Author)

A number of the wartime buildings at Weston-On-The-Green are put to good use.

Below: Skydive Weston's clubhouse *(Author)*

Below: overall view of the airfield, with a Dornier Skyservant off to the left.

Left: The parachute packing hall and training area in the T2 hangar *(Author)*

Below: JSAT sign 2006 *(Author)*

JSAT WESTON ON THE GREEN

PARACHUTE CENTRE

Right: One of the wartime air raid shelters. This shelter was removed after the crash of the Nomad in April 2002 *(Author)*

Below: HA-VOC waits another load at the emplaning point *(Author)*

Right: The original main gate about 250 m north of the current one *(Author)*

Below: An avtur bowser waits on the kite balloon mooring 'cartwheel' in 2007 with the warning sign for the departed Turbine Islander still present *(Author)*

WARNING
AVTUR
ONLY
G-WOTG

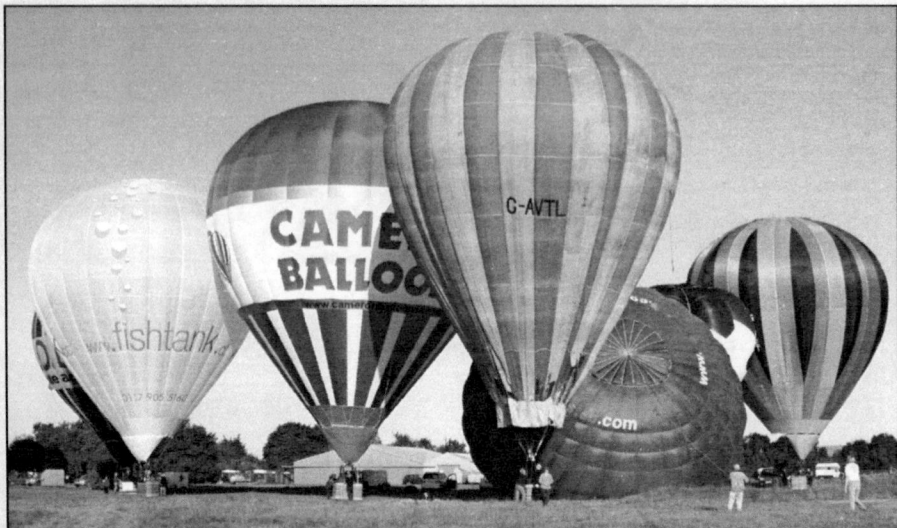

Above: On 9 July 2007 to commemorate the 40th anniversary of its first flight at Weston, G-AVTL takes centre stage at a gathering. (Bill Teasdale)

Left: *"Bristol Belle"* takes to the air at Weston once more on 9 July 2007 (Bill Teasdale)

Right: G-ODAY of the british Balloon Museum and Library about to get airborne at Weston. *(Bill Teasdale)*

Two views of a RAF C-130J Herculese making a weekend drop in August 2007 (Author)

Left: Entering the dome of the 1993 vintage operations block

Below: Another 1 PTS stick descending near the Operations block in August 2007
(both Author)

the interests of RAF skydivers.

During weekdays, the same facilities are used by the Joint Services Parachute Centre (Weston) which operates in a similar manner to the sister unit at Netheravon in Wiltshire.

To commemorate the 40th anniversary of the first flight of the "Bristol Belle" hot air balloon from Weston, on the morning of 9 July 2007 Don Cameron again made a flight across the airfield in the old lady. Eight other balloons were in attendance, some of which flew from the airfield. The previous evening there was an initial inflation for the benefit of a BBC camera man to record the occasion. Private aircraft are not encouraged but

Piper PA-22 G-ARIL was seen on 25 August and Beagle Pup G-AXDW on 20 October, both visiting Skydive Weston.

The Oxford Gliding Club which celebrated its 50th anniversary in August 2001 has now been in residence for more than 40 years and is still very active with a fleet of two K13s for initial training, two K8s for solo flying, a high performance DG-505 for cross country work and a T.21 for fun flying on warm days. The Glaser-Dirks DG-505 Orion is the latest addition to the fleet having been acquired in 2000. All gliders are winch launched but during any championships hosted by the OGC, tug aircraft are brought in from local clubs.

Due to the high level of parachuting carried out at Weston by the RAF and civilians, Danger Area D129 has been set up between Oxford and Bicester airfields into which no other aircraft are permitted. At weekends the OGC launch only when cleared to do so by the parachute DZ controller and keep clear of the Parachute Landing Area. Currently there are three runways and the OGC generally operate to the south or east, parachuting operating the other side of the airfield, the division being the active runway of the day. Although there has been recent speculation as to the future role of military parachuting, as long a 1 PTS remains at RAF Brize Norton, RAF Weston-on-the-Green will still have its part to play.

In preparation of this history I would like to thank Mike Westwood, Weston's Chief Pilot for his help and encouragement, the staff of 1 PTS, aviation historian Mike Gibson who's camera has missed very few visitors to the airfield over the years and John Norris, who made many military and civilian jumps at Weston for the use of his collection of Weston photos. Finally, much detailed information has been gleaned by reference to numerous Air-Britain publications.

Above: The Battle of Britain Memorial Flight's Dakota was used by 1 PTS on 23 May 2007*(Via Mike Westwood)*

Right: A weekend skydiver arriving above the manifest office *(Author)*

OFFICIAL & LOCAL NAME - WESTON-ON-THE-GREEN

COUNTY:	Oxfordshire	**AIRFIELD CODE:**	WG
LOCATION:	3.5 mls SW of Bicester	**LOCATION IND:**	????; EGZG
LANDMARKS:	Oxford-Bicester railway	**CONTL TOWER:**	type not known
	1.5 mls SE	**HANGARS**	2 x 9 bay, 2 x 12 bay, 1 xT2
GRID REF:	P985405(94)		2 double Blister, 6 single
LAT/LONG	51°52'45"N 01°13'15"W		Blister
HEIGHT ASL:	260ft	**RUNWAYS**	landing area
OBSTACLES:	Trees 30 ft on south	**HOUSING:**	none
	boundary	**OPENED :**	1918
LIGHTING:	none	**CLOSED :**	current

FLYING UNITS PRESENT AT WESTON-ON-THE-GREEN

UNIT	CODE	FROM	DATE IN	DATE OUT	TO	AIRCRAFT USED
28 TDS	-	(formed)	27.07.18	.03.19	(disbanded)	504, Camel, Salamander
2 Sqn	-	Bicester	.09.19	20.01.20	(disbanded)	FK.8
18 Sqn	-	Merheim	02.09.19	31.12.19	(disbanded)	In name only
90 Sqn	-	West Raynham	07.09.39	19.09.39	Upwood	Blenheim
101 Sqn	-	West Raynham	07.09.39	14.09.39	Brize Norton	Blenheim
2 GTS	-	Thame	08.12.41	10.03.43	(disbanded)	Audax, Hector, Hind, Hotspur, Master, Oxford, Proctor
130 GS	-	Abingdon	20.04.51	01.09.55	(disbanded)	Cadet, Dagling, Grunau. Sedbergh

UNITS THAT REGULARLY USED WESTON-ON-THE-GREEN

UNIT	FROM	DATE IN	DATE OUT	AIRCRAFT USED
04, 108 Sqns, 13 OTU	Bicester	.09.39	01.11.40	Anson, Blenheim
15 SFTS	Kidlington	01.11.40	21.02.42	Harvard, Oxford
20(P)AFU	Kidlington	06.04.43	21.06.45	Oxford, Anson, misc
1 PTS	Upper Heyford	15.03.46	10.06.50	Halifax, Dakota
1 PTS	Abingdon	.53	.01.76	Dakota, Beverley, Argosy, Hastings, Hercules
1 PTS	Brize Norton	.01.76	Current	Hercules, Skyvan
Oxford Gliding Club				
RAFSPA				
RAFGSA Chilterns Gliding Club				